REDUCE, REUSE, RECYCLE!

Garbage and Litter

Jen Green

PowerKiDS press.

New York

Published in 2010 by The Rosen Publishing Group Inc.
29 East 21st Street, New York, NY 10010

First Edition

Editor: Katie Powell
Designer: Elaine Wilkinson
Consultant: Kate Ruttle
Picture Researcher: Shelley Noronha
Photographer: Andy Crawford

Library of Congress Cataloging-in-Publication Data

Green, Jen.
  Garbage and litter / Jen Green.
     p. cm. -- (Reduce, reuse, recycle!)
  Includes index.
  ISBN 978-1-61532-234-3 (library binding)
  ISBN 978-1-61532-243-5 (paperback)
  ISBN 978-1-61532-244-2 (6-pack)
  1. Refuse and refuse disposal--Juvenile literature.
  2. Recycling (Waste, etc.)--Juvenile literature. I. Title.
  TD792.G737 2010
  363.72'8--dc22

                                2009023728

Photographs:
Cover: Stockbyte/Photolibrary. 1 Wayland Picture Library, 2 Altrendo Nature/Getty Images, 4 Ecoscene / photog,
5 Wayland Picture Library, 7 Banana Stock/jupiterimages/ImagePick, 8 & Cover Stockbyte/photolibrary.com,
9 Recycle Now, 10 Stockbyte/photolibrary.com, 11 Colin Seddon/Nature, 12 Wayland, 13 Altrendo Nature/Getty Images,
14 © Robert van der Hilst/CORBIS, 15 t, c, b ISTOCK,16 © Will & Deni McIntyre/CORBIS. 17 Wayland Picture Library,
18 Recycle Now, 19 © Don Mason/CORBIS, 20, 21 Wayland Picture Library, 22 Recycle Now, 23, 24, 25, 26, 27
Ecoscene / photog, 28 l & r Wayland, 29 r Wayland, 29 l & b Recycle Now

With thanks to RecycleNow.

The author and publisher would like to thank the following models: Sam Mears and Madhvi Paul.

Manufactured in China
CPSIA Compliance Information: Batch #WAW0102PK: For Further Information
contact Rosen Publishing, New York, New York at 1-800-237-9932

Contents

Words in **bold** can be found in the glossary.

The problem of waste

Each week, you and your family produce at least one trash can full of garbage. With all the people in the world, that makes a huge amount of waste. Getting rid of garbage is a problem. It is building up in garbage dumps and in the natural world to harm our planet and its wildlife.

▲ *In many countries, garbage is collected each week by truck.*

We can all help to solve the problem of garbage by following the three R's—**reduce**, **reuse**, and **recycle**. Reducing means using less of something. Reusing means using something again. Recycling is when garbage is used to make a new product.

▶ *Garbage contains useful* **materials** *that can be recycled.*

What's in the can?

Have you ever thought about what goes in your trash can? Every week, people throw away newspapers, magazines, and leftover food. Some people also put cans, glass bottles, plastic containers, old clothes, toys, and worn-out machinery in the garbage.

▼ *This pie chart shows the amounts of different kinds of trash people threw away in the United States, in 2008.*

Yard waste & food scraps 45%

Containers & packaging 28%

Durable items eg appliances & furniture 10%

Non-durable items eg newspapers & clothes 17%

▶ **Fast food** such as pizza comes with a lot of packaging, which is often just thrown away.

You Can Help!

Find out how much waste your family throws away each week. Make a chart with headings such as "Food waste" and "Plastic." Keep a record of what items are thrown away. Are you able to reduce the amount of garbage?

A lot of what we throw away is packaging—the wrappings of the things we buy. Packaging can help to protect things, but often it just makes them look bright and colorful. Packaging is made from materials such as paper, cardboard, and plastic, which could be reused.

Mountains of garbage

All the garbage we throw away has to be put somewhere. A lot gets dumped in **landfill sites**. Some is burned in very hot **furnaces** called **incinerators**. But gases from these furnaces can **pollute** the air.

◄ A truck dumps waste at a landfill site. Sometimes waste leaks out of the dump to pollute the air, water, and soil.

People in different countries produce different amounts of garbage. A family in the United States makes seven times as much garbage as a family in India.

Garbage dumped in landfill sites is squashed and buried. Eventually, the landfill site gets full. Many countries are running out of places to put these dumps. Some garbage is dumped at sea, where it can harm wildlife.

◄ At the store, choose products with less packaging. That way, there is less garbage to throw away.

9

A lot of litter

Litter is garbage that gets dropped instead of being put in a trash can. Litter clutters cities and spoils the beauty of the countryside. It can also harm wildlife. For example, animals such as birds and seals can die if they swallow or get tangled up in plastic.

◀ Dumped litter spoils the look of the countryside.

◀ *Small animals can get trapped in the plastic rings used to hold soda cans.*

LITTER SURVEY

1. Find a place near you where litter is a problem—for example, your school playground or a park.

2. What types of litter have been left—is it paper, food waste, packaging, or dumped machinery?

3. Make a chart with headings such as "Food Waste," "Plastic," and "Packaging." Send your chart to your **local authority** and ask them to plan a cleanup.

You Can Help!

Ask your teacher to plan a class trip to clean up a local park or beauty spot. Remember to wear gloves.

Will it rot?

Some kinds of garbage **rot** more quickly than others. **Natural** materials, such as food, paper, and yard waste, rot quite quickly. Fruit and vegetables can be recycled on the **compost** pile. They make a good **fertilizer** for a garden plot.

▶ *These fruit and vegetable peelings have started to rot in just a few days.*

Paper takes about a month to rot. Wool and cloth take about a year. Tin cans take about 300 years, plastic about 450 years. Glass does not rot.

Man-made materials, such as plastic, glass, and metal, take longer to **decay**. If they are dropped on the ground, they will stay the same for hundreds of years.

▼ *Plastic, metal, and glass last a long time, harming the natural world.*

13

Reduce, reuse, recycle

Everyone can help to solve the problem of waste. The first thing to do is to reduce the amount of garbage you throw away. Can you share or borrow things instead of buying them? Reuse paper, glass jars, and plastic bags. Can broken things be repaired?

▶ In some countries, such as Tunisia, people repair things instead of throwing them away.

Recycling is when glass, metal, and other materials are saved and used either to make the same thing or something new. In some areas, the local authority collects materials for recycling from homes. In others, we can take them to a **recycling center**.

▶Look for these symbols to help you decide what to do with your garbage.

You Can Help!

Separate materials for recycling such as glass, paper, and plastic. Rinse containers to make sure they are clean.

Bottles and jars

Every family in the United States throws away at least one glass bottle or jar a week. Glass can be recycled. It can also be reused, for example, old bottles can hold candles or flowers. Jelly jars make great pencil pots!

◄ *In some countries, different colors of glass go into different recycling bins. Never throw glass. Just place it gently in the bin.*

Glass is made by heating sand and **limestone** in a furnace at a very high temperature. This uses a lot of **energy**. Glass can easily be recycled. Bottles and jars are crushed and reheated at a lower temperature to make new glass. Recycling glass saves energy and **raw** materials.

Did You Know?

Making recycled glass uses less energy than making fresh glass. In some countries, such as Sweden, people often return glass bottles to be refilled.

Food and beverage cans

Food cans are made of a material called steel. Beverage cans are made from aluminum. These metals are made from **minerals** dug from the ground and heated in a furnace. This uses up a lot of energy and causes **pollution**.

▶ *Cans can be squashed using a can crusher, before taking them to a recycling point.*

Food and beverage cans are difficult to reuse, but they are easy to recycle. The used cans are reheated, melted, and molded to make new ones. Recycling cans saves energy and cuts pollution.

▶ Most of the cans you see in the supermarkets contain some recycled metal.

Paper and cardboard

We throw away a lot of paper and cardboard. This includes mail, newspapers, books, and a lot of packaging. Paper and cardboard are made from wood **pulp**, which is made from trees. Paper and cardboard are easy to recycle.

◄ *Used newspaper can be shredded and mixed with water to make a mushy pulp. This is rolled thin to make recycled paper.*

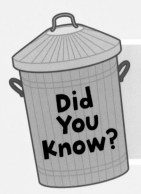

Making five tons of recycled paper (this is the same weight as an elephant) can save up to 85 trees.

TIPS FOR REDUCING WASTE AND REUSING PAPER

1. You can reduce paper waste by asking the post office to stop delivering **junk mail** to your home.

2. Use both sides of paper to write on. Print on both sides of the paper, too.

3. Reuse old envelopes using tape.

4. You can also reuse wrapping paper if you open your presents carefully.

▼ You can recycle old birthday and Christmas cards to make great gift tags!

The problem with plastic

Toys, clothes, packaging, and cars can be made using plastic. So can glue, paint, and plastic bags. There are many types of plastic, such as nylon, which is used in clothing, and polystyrene, used in foam packaging. All are made from oil using a lot of energy.

◀ Buy one large plastic bottle of soda and refill it instead of buying lots of small ones.

Plastic is light and strong but it rots very slowly, which makes it a problem to get rid of. When it is burned, it can give off a **poisonous** gas. Plastic can be recycled to make all kinds of useful things, from fleece jackets and sleeping bags, to crates and furniture. You can also reuse plastic pots and tubs as containers.

► *This fleece jacket has been made from recycled plastic.*

Did You Know?

We use 20 times more plastic today than people did 50 years ago.

Dealing with plastic

Recycling plastic is expensive because the many different types all have to be sorted and recycled separately. For this reason, it is better to reduce the amount of plastic you waste.
You can also reuse plastic.
For example, reuse plastic bags when you go shopping.

◀ Take a cloth bag when you go shopping, so you don't need plastic bags at all.

TIPS FOR REDUCING PLASTIC WASTE

1. Choose food in paper cartons or glass bottles rather than plastic containers.

2. Avoid using plastic plates, cups, and cutlery. Use ordinary ones that can be washed and used again.

▼ You can buy unpackaged fruit and vegetables at a farmers' market.

FRUITS
ET LEGUMES
BIOLOGIQUES
D'AQUITAINE

Clothes, toys, and machinery

People have always bought clothes as new styles come into fashion. Nowadays, we also want new cell phones and computers, and the latest toys and games. We sometimes throw away old things that could still be used. Old clothes, books, and toys can all be sold, for example, at **thrift stores**.

◀ *Charity thrift stores sell secondhand clothes and books to raise money for people in need.*

▶ *Flea markets and yard sales are great places to sell any unwanted items.*

REUSING AND RECYCLING

1. Ask your family to find out if faulty machinery can be repaired rather than thrown away.

2. Some stores that sell cell phones will take your old one to be reused or recycled.

3. Plan a "swap shop" at school to sell your stuff and get new things.

4. You could sell any unwanted items at a yard sale or give them to a rummage sale.

Start a compost pile

Start a compost pile for food waste and yard trimmings. Putting compost on the garden plot helps plants and vegetables grow strong and healthy.

YOU WILL NEED:

- an ice-cream tub,
- a sponge,
- a compost pile or bin outside—you can buy a plastic compost bin from your local authority or garden center.

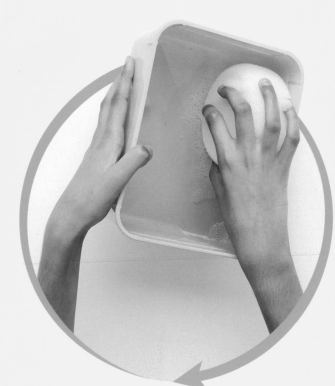

1. Reuse an old ice-cream tub. Wash it using dish detergent.

2. Wearing gloves, sort your garbage. Dead flowers, fruit and vegetable peelings, yard waste, and shredded paper can all be put on the compost pile. Don't put meat scraps or cooked food on the pile.

3. Put the sorted garbage into your ice-cream tub. Replace the lid.

4. When the tub is full, ask an adult to put the contents onto the compost pile or bin outside.

5. In just three months, rich compost will be ready to put on your garden plot.

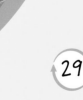

29

Further Information and Web Sites

Topic map

GEOGRAPHY

Contact your local authority to find out the location of local landfill sites and recycling centers. Find them on a map.

SCIENCE

Use a magnet to check whether cans are made from steel or aluminum. Steel is magnetic, aluminum is not.

ART/DESIGN

Cardboard tubes and plastic tubs and trays can be used in craft projects. Use shredded paper to make papier mâché to mold figures and masks.

ENGLISH

Write a report on why it's important to reduce, reuse, and recycle. Or write a story about recycling from the point of view of a glass bottle or soda can!

HISTORY

Find out when paper, glass, steel, and plastic were first invented using the Internet or a local library.

MATH

Sell some items at a yard sale. Put price tags on your things, and make sure you give people the right change. Add up all the money you make at the sale.

Further reading

Environment Action: Recycle by Kay Barnham (Crabtree Publishing, 2007)
Reducing and Recycling Waste by Carol Inskipp (Gareth Stevens Publishing, 2005)
Reducing Garbage by Sue Barraclough (Sea to Sea Publications, 2007)
Waste and Recyling by Sally Morgan (Smart Apple Media, 2006)

Web Sites

Due to the changing nature of Internet links, PowerKids Press has developed an online list of Web sites related to the subject of this book. This site is updated regularly. Please use this link to access this list:
http://www.powerkidslinks.com/reduce/garbage/

Glossary

compost	natural materials that rot to make fertilizer for plants
decay	to rot or to spoil
energy	the power to do work
fast food	ready-made food, which you can buy and eat right away
fertilizer	a substance added to the soil to make plants grow more easily
furnace	a hot oven in which things are burned
incinerator	a very hot furnace in which garbage is burned
junk mail	mail that is delivered to many homes to advertise businesses
landfill site	a garbage dump, where waste is buried underground
limestone	a rock that is used to make glass
local authority	the organization that runs services such as waste collection in your area
man-made	something made that is not found naturally
material	something used to make something else
mineral	a non-living natural substance
natural	something that is found naturally
poisonous	a substance that can make you sick if you swallow or sometimes touch it
pollute	when harmful materials dirty the air, water, or soil
pollution	when harmful material gets into the air, water, or soil
pulp	a mushy mixture
raw	a natural material such as wood
recycle	when garbage is saved and remade into a new product
recycling center	a center where waste materials are recycled
reduce	to make something smaller or use less of it
reuse	when something is used again
rot	when a substance breaks down
thrift store	a store that sells secondhand items to raise money, usually for a good cause

Index

Numbers in **bold** refer to a photograph.